MW01278014

The Window Ledge

Also by R. E. Smith

A Sweeter Understanding

The Window Ledge

R. E. SMITH

R.E. Smith

Sofa Ink

Vancouver, Washington

The Window Ledge
by R. E. Smith

10 digit ISBN: 0-9769261-3-X
13 digit ISBN: 978-0-9769261-3-9

Edited by Linda M. Meyer.

Cover design by Belle Larsen.
Author photos by Jennifer Lydick. Reproduced by
permission. www.longstofly.com.
Interior design by David Cowsert.

Printed and bound in the United States.

Sofa Ink
PO Box 65849
Vancouver, WA 98665
www.sofaink.com

10 09 08 07 06   1 2 3 4 5

For those who encouraged my ascent to the position of poet and author, I must offer sincere appreciation. To those who offered kind words and caring criticism, you have helped me construct the vehicle of words for the journey. You are all a part of the language of verses that connect us in the vignettes designed by my perspective of the world in which we live. For those who have displayed and shared love and friendship, your examples are immortalized in my work. To all of you, please accept my humble thanks.

— R. E. Smith

Table of Contents

Preface

I believe poetry is not only the music of our souls,
it is the symphonies of who and what we are. It
defines our memories, our dreams, and wishes.
Poetry connects us to the tones and colors and
sweet recollection of our past, present, and future.

   Poetry is also the universal language of emotion,
desire, and regret. It is our collective hope, the
world of experience, and all the loves we can
possibly share.

   As we make our journeys through life, poetry
leads us to revelations we cannot imagine ahead
of time. It helps us define how we touch or are
touched by the world around us. It is meant to
last a moment, a lifetime, or an eternity in the
universal message of understanding. It also helps
document what is right or wrong in our sphere of
influence.

   This is my definition of what poetry is. It would
please me to have you agree with or adopt some
or all of what you read here, as an affirmation
that you share my vision as well as the world of
my perspective and the journey we are about
to embark upon. We are about to cross over the
window ledge into the world of my imagination.
Welcome aboard and enjoy the trip.

— *R. E. Smith*

Acknowledgments

I am deeply grateful to my publisher and friend, David Cowsert. His vision of developing my work into a wonderful gift book has meant personal and professional sacrifice as well as a commitment of time and resources. The results have far exceeded my expectations.

I am aware that it is the editor's job to make the writer look better. I must confess that Linda Meyer, editor of my work, has shown amazing talent in helping develop my poetry and in providing me with confidence as a writer. She shows great insight when making suggestions that strengthen the poems in form and meaning. I am eternally in her debt.

The support and encouragement of my family and friends continue to flow freely. It has been a pleasure meeting so many new people at the readings and book signings who have been kind in their comments and quick to join the entourage of supporters wishing me future success. This book is for all of you with my personal thanks for accepting me into your world as a versifier. I will continue to reward your faith with humility, while striving for excellence in my work.

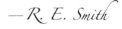

— R. E. Smith

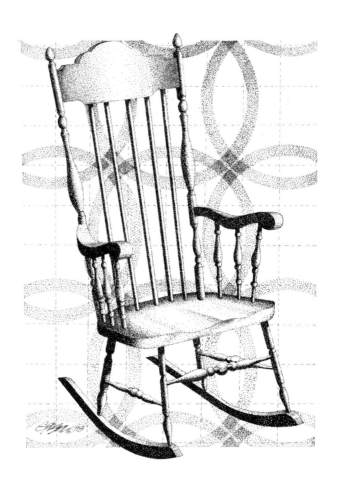

hopeful revision

The road of love
often turns
painfully from the direction we choose
but rarely
disappears from view.
For we are the journey
that wanders briefly across
this well-traveled bridge of life.
As pain and joy intersect
as tears and promises fall
hope revives
the spirit of the trip
as together again
lights the brooding darkness
beyond the disappearing unknown.

night light

Voices soft and so appealing
tell us what the night's revealing.
Does the candle's flame intrude
upon the night so dark and rude?
Or does its light protect, keep out
surrounding blackness from without?
Is it not what seems to be?
Or is the dark deluding me?
Does the flicker dance about
to keep people in, or empty out?

Though I like to think of my writing and your reading as a
shared activity, it occurred to me not to interrupt your reading
with tidbits from my mind. Yet in these small notes, I invite you
to share more deeply with me and I with you. In this way, we
are both enriched. Unlike many face-to-face encounters, this
book allows us each to explore at whim—skipping, rereading,
or considering at our convenience. Thank you for sharing this
journey with me.

— R. E. S.

wellborn

I am
wellborn.
My world of luxury is
my friends
my loves
and peace of mind.

I know...I know.

rainy days

Wind, rain blowing in my face
distort the view like curtain lace
on all things done, both large and small
that first I tried and now recall.

Time elopes with youth departed
taking along moods once started
so much joy, now lost in pain
that once was love is now disdain.

Where then did the blurring start?
If not the mind, then in the heart.
Direction danced on fickle feet
while music shared its own deceit.

Now locked behind decisions passed
sorting out the die first cast
adversity frowns at memory's lies
where lightening struck, the karma cries.

I wonder aloud if storms intend
to signal meaning to the end
of wind, rain blowing in my face
contained within that curtain lace.

Tears of a lost love can distort rational explanations or suggest more difficult questions to answer. We can all get momentarily lost in the confusion of sorting out the part we played. It is just another step in learning to deal with life experiences, even the bad ones. Life is, after all, always a work in progress.

— R. E. S.

the water's edge

Dusk settles
around the afternoon of life
and to the softest voice of memory clings
listening for
the indulging interlude of escape
offered by shackled bonds of time
which fall free
from the insurgent tide of thought.
This swinging gate of leisure
returns us
to the oceans of our experience
where the spring of youth
found us grazing hungrily
from ticking fields of time
as we tread precariously close
to lingering winds of rapture
found undulating
near the water's edge of understanding.

half and half

Love
is a kind word
forgiving smile
warm hand
gentle touch
the thought of you
I hear so much
that tells me love
is more than real.
It's what I see
and what I feel.
Love is here
before my eye
it's one half you
and one half I.

a work in progress

Our love is a work in progress.
As such it always will be
defining emotions and feelings
all it means to you, and to me.

Our relationship sags like a vintage house
weathered by elements and time.
Shingles are blown from the well-worn roof
victims of your wind and mine.

The message contained in so much of our prattle
pulls hard on emotional beams
drawn hard over lips of interminable battle
destroying our hopes and our dreams.

The walls of our structure are searching for paint
like a hug so desperate for arms.
Our trim isn't pretty, actually cracking with pity
having long ago lost all its charms.

Some say the house that we fashioned in pleasure
is beginning to sag from more than just weather.
Our relationship changed as dreams fell apart
and the aging occurred with each broken heart.

From the well-laden shelves of a marriage now broken
is there anything left here to save?
To go on pretending is an emotional token
turning each of us into a slave.

Yet giving in is defining our work still in progress
outlining the reasons for staying
or confining our lessons hard-learned by the fights
just to keep us from straying.

To affirm the commitment, to strengthen the sag
to weather the relationship's storm
let's start with the hug, finish with pleasure
and get back to what once was the norm.

lonely

The mountain stretched
its craggy face
to yawn across the earthen grace
setting my thoughts
in a motion of space
to fall lost
on a moment of lonely
disappearing as quietly
as the butterfly's breath
against the morning mist
swift and quiet
as a falling star
before it hits the disappearing
unknown darkness.
The walk of yesterday's love
becomes tomorrow's memory of life.

communicate

There are parallel designs
in every cup of smiles
each a mirror of thought and motion
both a catalyst and reaction of the other
for the fleeting moment
we are communication.

divided emotions

I drink from the well of
    experience
but my mouth remains blatantly dry.
I eat from the table of
    happiness
yet all I do is cry.
I read from the book of
    knowledge
and still can't find my way.
I wish from the mountain of
    dreams
but hope doesn't brighten my day.
I wonder when my light turned to
    want
where darkness was waiting for me.
I followed a map to find
    feelings
but Braille doesn't help me to see.
No mountain of dreams brings you
    near
the painful anguish I feel
releasing the grip of my
    longing
to revive promise stolen from me.

eternal hope

Life is an evening walk
through Nature's own resounding chorus
of talking leaves and crisp breezes
that prompt lovers to snuggle
against the wind of each other
and doze in the comfort of
Indian summer evenings
with hope as the fire
dominating an open hearth
to stave the bite of winter's frigid mouth
and preserve the dream of warm tomorrows.

springtime

The shadowed boundary
of faceless waters...
Life's tuning fragrance
fills blossoms with
relentless images of
love lost
awakens drowsy flowers
from winter's sleepy grasp
placing budding stems
in spring's awakened hand.

autumn's moment

The summer naught beside the earth
plants deciding now to hide
leaves departed from the trees
their colors fading doth subside.
Quickened senses gathering in
the season's mood of change
imagination stirs the soup
of memory's widest range.
Ingredients mixed of past and present
preparing tomorrow for winter's ride
the thought of loving youthful treasures
warm the heart then push aside.

the purpose

The sea must wait
the ebbing tide
to crest the twining shore
with waves to hold
the balances, between each rise and fall.

The sky holds close
each cloud's moment
of precious flight
of tireless wandering
to protect, the vanquished empty from its view.

The earth grows tired
for its burden
is great, and restless grows
the motion of its way
but settles, within its own relinquished need.

Love is patient
and finds its reward
in the returning attention
of each echo our voices
prepare, in the shadow of creation's purpose.

i am who i am

I am common and yet I'm not.
I am special but not a lot.
I am different, so aren't we all?
But I am me, most of all.

I have given what I've received.
And if I am what is perceived
then I am you in work and play
and we are one in every way.

There is no manner from which to discern
what we know from what we learn
until the moment we must do
that which separates the me from you.

Contained within the pain and grief
is the emergence of renewed belief
that once we seek the bottom line
I'll still be me, though you're not mine.

I'll still be common and better for it.
I'll still be special in a different way
the difference apparent to one and all
I'll still be me, most of all.

weakness

Of the most disappointing
   adventures in life
   few can be more depressing
   than when you must admit
   that the power of your ability
   is less than
   the extension of your reach.

black angel

Angel wrapped
in bed of thorn
measure time by every smile
as darkness starts
to breach the earth
it cautions every mile.
The constant noise
of growing grass
beneath the mortals' feet
another form
to fill and serve
history to repeat.
To judge yourself
would not be fair
even though you must
for if they call
you rush to hear
the price so cruel, unjust.
Repeat your sleep
in bed of thorn
knowing all the while
until you find
your own soft cloud
keep looking for the smile.

the blanket

There is peace to seek within the rain
prevailing in a constant wind
as it skitters down our rooftop drain
beyond what conscious dreams offend
emotion's storm of wretched truth
layered in protective pain.

There are shades designed within such passion
that dissipate storms' torrential loss
colored long on feeling, exempt compassion
past images wrapped about our cross.
Cloth to bind our past and present
woven in such knotted fashion.

Only time sufficient will help explain
having served as faithful every season
how memories depart in shocked disdain
etched on walls first caged in reason.
The blanket of congruence folded.
Peace confined within the rain.

kitten-soft

Sometimes there is a mood in me
      that's kitten-soft and furry.
It happens every now and then
      but never causes worry.
The theme throughout the way I feel
      has much to do with you.
When you are close, I sense the need
      to crawl within your view.
As you reach out to draw me near
      my inner self does purr.
You pet my neck or scratch my ear
      and worry starts to blur.
You'll always have my heartfelt thanks
      for treating me this way
'cause when you stroke the mood in me
      it always makes my day.
So if the place that's kitten-soft
      is ever on your mind
I'll purr until the mood is gone
      in hopes that you'll be mine.

the earthen plow

You are the stars that fill my sky of life
the raindrops on my shore
a ray of hope from brilliant days
the wind against my door.
You mix for me moods deep-felt
like clouds prepare a rain
then smile to light my dark of life
to make me whole again.

You wrap a certain childish charm
with wisdom's vapor spread
ego of my ocean's wave
if only in my head.
To fill the void where lonely dwelled
its memory dimming now
because of you the earth in me
accepts your earthen plow.

Like so many of you, I have gone through moments of loss and had to learn to deal with it while trying to salvage parts of myself. This poem shows the influence of a caring love who helped bolster me through the darkness until I could stand erect in the world of tragic experience.

— R. E. S.

quasi modo geniti infantes

People weeping
slowly keeping
feelings moving
soon revealing
comfort zones
like shrouds concealing
emotional tones
beyond repealing.

pleasurable haunting

I can't sleep
while you keep
running through my head.
Your smile alone
or eyes that stare
laughter soft
your thoughts are there.
You keep me up!
Why not instead
come sleep with me
in my warm bed?

on and on and on

Bright as a well-dressed morning
quiet as the sleeping dawn
fresh as spring's beginning
my love for you goes on.
So follow me into the night of life
into dusk where our thoughts blend
to watch the shadows rise and fall
where our dreams will never end.

words

When I express what you mean to me
  profess undying love
  swear by stars in heaven
  moonlight up above
  share a vision of the future
  where we stroll hand in hand
  around our dreams and back again
  sharing love's delicate plan.
Let your heart dance with every note
  of music I describe
  as a melody plays in all we do.
If finally we decide
  to walk through life
  as one instead of two
  you'll begin to feel life's harmony
  watching over you.
Of all these things that I might say
  so you'll believe in me
  our love will last beyond just words
  but you should clearly see.
Words are all I may ever have
  to steal your heart away
  erasing doubts that others express
  about what I do or say.

This poem was inspired by a Bee Gees' song entitled "Words." It is dedicated to them in honor of Maurice Gibbs, who passed away in 2003.

— R. E. S.

the window ledge

The view from the window so depends
on which perspective we each lend
to what is seen that moves about
or that which somehow lingers stout
within ourselves in truth or feeling
as we strain to see the moment's meaning.

Sweeping free the dust embodied
molecules congregate, distorting light.
A vision darkened by passing time
not yet made clear or resolute
cannot reach through emotional panes
to cleanse the other side of understanding.

So to lean against the window ledge
the forehead cools, in temperate wedge
as tears excite the dust discovered
puddle in the thoughts uncovered
demanding truth, revealing doubt
whether gazing in or looking out.

*My editor's comments eloquently express what the poem is
all about. "I have always appreciated this poem, thus the book's
title choice. I can see dust motes drifting in the shaft of sunlight
from the spot on the window wiped clean of dirt. It is a tangible
representation of emotional duality—both sides of what should
be a clear window, yet a deceptive lack of clarity."*
— *R. E. S.*

28

suffering

Do not surround me with
what went wrong
when the room was empty
darkness suppressing.
Do not disavow me
because I love you
or because you think
I do not.
I am suffering
in my own way
a casualty of
suffocating expressions
of tomorrow's lonely wail.

Rissa

Laughter begged his attention
touched an ear softly
whispered directions for his gaze
to rest upon her beautiful smile.
The menu flashed brilliantly.
Believe in magic! Believe in me!
The tattered, dirty tablecloth curled its edges
became a blanket on the sandy beach where
he now stood looking at her.
The muse sang to him from some distant shore.
The plank flooring and barn-wood walls became
sunshine coaxing him closer to her.
Cloaked in her flirtatious glance, he paused.
Naw, I couldn't be this lucky, he thought.
Doubt crowded him, bringing with it the taste of stale beer
and the sour sound of raucous music.
Looking at the menu, "Coca-cola with no ice," he said
to the waiter, "Nothing more."
When he looked up at last, she was gone.
Her chair stood empty against the wall, lonely against the
memory of her.
Not once had he moved from the table.
But this magic would always perplex him.
He lost more than confidence when she disappeared.
Life was forever diminished for him by his loss.
He never found the woman of his dream
and compared all others to the fading vision of her.

genealogy at a glance

Time and distance
pull at the skin of procrastinators
giving them unreasonable purpose
for delaying almost anything.

Space and motion
bend the bones of lovers
helping them in their pursuit
of being together at all costs.

Reason and reasonableness
round up the masses
providing purpose to lives
in the curve of affability.

For the rest of the population
there is a certain accouchement
releasing them from any paradigm
as it relates to their own forbearance.

in the beginning

I've stood in the dark
to see dawn settle day
in night's awakened shadow.
Waited to dry while outgrowing
my need of the sea.
Assumed sand as my own.
Without vision I'd certainly be
all of which would be nothing
without you, without me.

love lost

The bed
still warm
from where you lay
to awaken me
in rescue from
life's most vicious nightmare
of losing you.
The foreboding chill
descends
as the mattress
gives up your form
returning me
to nightmare's grasp
strangled and suffocated
by the reality of
your no longer being there.

love seeks its own

Time-tempered love
never lost
but carried carefully
in quiet corners of consciousness
is salvaged
in moments of recognition
as couplets of
life's poetic interlude.

For those of you
who do not know
or are too blind to see
leave love alone
to seek its own
for it will truly be.

For the deaf
who refuse to hear
the truth of beauty found
all sound of love
I sadly fear
will fall upon the ground.

The muted few
who just condemn
or shame us with your hand
your voice will heal
to emptiness
your mind, return to sand.
The few who feel
the wind of love
pushing at the tree
have pity for
the deaf and dumb
for they will always be.

adulthood

I have the room now
to decide things.
I found it
within my own expanse.
I have the capacity now
to understand
it's always been there
lurking in my subconscious.
I know you better now
than ever before
because I know myself
and confidence restored.
I haven't changed
from what I've been
I have grown
because I am still learning.

*It is an amazing feeling when we realize we are in control of
our lives. Once we grow beyond our own restrictions, we can
become masters of our own destinies. Even while we continue to
learn and apply the lessons of new experience in a life we often
have difficulty understanding.*

— R. E. S.

love's design

I walked
across the room of life
to search
the light of day
only to find
the approaching night
filled
with the lamp of what
we had already shared
as we strolled together
in the burdensome obedience
of love's design.

symbiosis

Tomorrow will be
a happier place for us
as a memory
or reality
because either way
we'll always be together
for there is no way
to separate the sunshine
from its warmth
and so we'll still be one.

boredom

Boredom is the hungriest seed
of all emotions.
       It lacks taste as a meal
       and beauty as a weed
for it is wasting
even as it grows.
       It leans against productive fields
       choking even sunflowers
as it transmits, empty
where lamps of knowing once existed.

Ponder not the pause
of its existence or demise
       for knowing it
       will have brought you there.
Feeling it
will startle its departure.
       Its tongue will feed
       upon the motion of soul
to cancer bones of existence once portrayed
and the affirmative action wondering once supplied.

friends

If you wonder who I am or why
it may help you to know me as one
who would like to be everything
you'd ever expect from a friend.
Always in a hurry to know you
never wanting to forget.
Waiting to share the pleasure you give
wishing to spoil you when least expected
and hoping you smile when I've pleased you.
I like you just because you are.
Because you are, I am.

musical score

Light in the absence of sound.
Stars surrendering night
in musical memories of unscored tune
unfurled by love's soft hand
to wave generously in the wind of you.
The sun will shine brighter now
on the garden's flowers
because your smile
rested briefly in its view.

blush of winter rose

I see your radiance
   and settle in the glow you've created.
Share your dreams
   of fireplaces, snowdrifts
      and love's gentle touch
         where whispers drift buoyantly
            on each wish's shadow.
I live to kiss the blushing freshness
   of knowing you fulfilled
      and delight
         in watching flowers grow envious
            of winter's solitary rose.

together again in desert heat

Noiseless quiet transcends
desert heat
with filling thoughts of love.
Empty arms and full desire
my need, my loneliness
travel alone to meet you.
The journeys end
where they begin
in streets of your first smile
in our hello
in love's beginning.

institution of man

Where minds unite discussion with
expression's final form
to bridge the tentative gaps between
        theory, reality, emotion, and dreams

Where old and new are habits sorted
whose dialogues touch conclusions and
        life begins, again and again

Where confidence, in shadows grows
on abstract's plebian eminence
direction's color determined
forms history's glorious moments of prologue
to summon tomorrow's thinkers
        into an even more uncertain future.

Where at once raconteurs chant
Magna est veritas et prevalebit.
To which the apostates, in common, reply
Noli me tangere, inter alia; cherchez la femme, and
        life begins, again and again.

44

the lover's mirror

Today is
the mirror of yesterday
with reflections
slow to change.
Tonight cities will sleep
in magic shadows
of twinkling light
that disturbs
the latent evening glare
and the sated moment
of together again.

renewal

Take time to feel
the world revolve
around dedicated merging
of tomorrow's silhouettes
and from the renewed spirit
grow free
in the surrounding optimism
of limitless youthful dreams.

secrets

Walls that live within us
are only empty spaces
filled with secret words
thoughts of names and places
of times soon past
related to the events
of each other
never known again
except in separate memory.

noster amor aeternale

— our love is eternal

June 20, 1976

From these cups your lives will pour.
Drink of the knowledge that love can satisfy your thirst.
Keep them filled with yourselves, so others may be refreshed
by the example of your creation.
Fill them often with dreams of tomorrow
so sharing becomes commonplace.
Make each taste a habit of truth
so you will not dine a moment alone.
Then when you grow wise in the approaching evening of life
you will see reflected in memory's vision
all you promised on this day of commitment to each other.

midnight's empty smile

Heaven reveals its quieting midnight smile
anesthetizing my loneliness.
Dreams to fulfill a wish
become the breeze that belongs to love
sighing from within a memory.
The songs of yesterday are empty rooms
upon the musical score of muted thought.
Reality breaks beaming through windows of the morning
then missing you is no longer such a dark surprise.

argument's demise

Nothing can bring the cold
and icy war of words
to a quicker end
than the professionalism of
a single pillow
on a double bed.

the grand insignificance

Feeling like a walk
on a brilliant sunny day
up a staircase
over Nature's paths and
concrete streets and sidewalks
into the universe.
We are of such little consequence
reminding us, that as a walk
we may only be gone
for an immeasurably short time.

man in the bigger scheme of things

There is a countenance
a covenant
from One to another
directed
protected
by God and by man.
In Spirit
the Being
competes without seeing
sees
knows
and knowing weeps
unseen
aware
that man's weakness is
competing
completing
the countenance
a covenant
from One to another
that God is Supreme
and man is, after all
just man.

the rush of anticipation

When I look at the mountains
I am absorbed into their mass.
When I look at the clouds
I am elevated to new heights.
When I reach out to the crowd
I become a part of it.
When I think about you
I feel revived
as refreshed
as clean air feels to a desperate breath.
When I look into the ocean of blue
I see your eyes looking back at me too.
And when I climb the stairs at night
my hopes invariably grow
with the rise and fall of footsteps
leading me closer to your door.

the eternal optimist

Why must the absence of loving
be so profound that it
storms on the joy of memories
left behind?
Is it because love is everything
and that is the price to pay?
If my dues are called
I would gladly give
so the purchase of softer memories
could temporarily exist without emptiness.
So that love could go on with or without me.
So that love could go on, and so, therefore, could I.

season of painted tears

Love nourished in wooded shade
on darkened green, in summer
where paths escaped noiselessly.
Love blossomed as sunshine peeked
through slick leaves
drinking heartily the moisture of diminishing clouds.
Love grew in its own right
above dry earth and parched grass
walked through and lived with
each birdcall, wildflower
broken promise, and disappointment
while time withdrew.
Love was a rainbow.
Autumn discovered its brilliance
second best, moving trees to cry.
Each leaf, a painted tear that fell.
Less light and more cold.
Winter's truth chased lovers
indoors
to watch again for love and spring.

touching the real you

I'm sorry when I touch your past
that it feels like someone real
pushing buttons of uncertainty
that time has yet to heal.

I wonder why, when you speak of them
your eye contains a tear
as if the storm of times gone by
mingles old and new, in fear.

Do clouds disrupt a gentleness
you need to know is there
with both hands nearly touching you
embraced by what we share?

In time the pause will be enough
to sleep away those dreams.
In sleep you'll find apology
with strength sewn in the seams.

Let hope, the gentle breeze, repeal
the moment of your fright
caress the corners of your heart
as a candle blesses night.

With friends restore the confidence
your smile can be your shield
'til love is the entire world you know
until the pain is healed.

And in the bitter cleft of heart
where the past is finally done
incorporate your energy
the best is yet to come.

mask of tomorrow

Evening smiles
upon reposing light
and dresses night
in retiring shadows
until the faceless voice
of a nameless face
yawns in the ear
of tomorrow's reality.

the sad, sad circus

The earth in full view
preserved
by so few
lying
dying
protecting
electing.
Laws to break laws.
Man to break men
no longer a friend.
Booing
while viewing.
Never paying
a price of admission.
Some circus of life
we all must attend.

altered states

I shall sleep
   and in my darkness dream
   while in the dream to weep
   to find hope
   that you'll be near
   when at last I awaken
   to have you find me here
   knowing you *will* find me here
I shall awaken.

sky parades

Earth against the angry sky
streams of sunshine in momentary splendor.
Heavy rain following a roaring wind
whose droplets rush to slap the ground.
Gentler clouds seek the silver lining
each in place, parading decorously
arriving in time, dressed as a lady
perfuming senses, summer her balm.

the way you are

The breath of spring bends the night
with a whispered message
of flowers and scented rain
that speaks of tomorrow
and memories
of promise
and promises of memories
using your name to say
"Smile, summer's coming
with bare arms
windblown hair
and love."

my favorite time of year

On the first day of summer
we have a chance to be
the words of every love song
and the promise they foresee.

In autumn when leaves brighten
lovers are ablaze
filling up with passion
hoping winter's chill to stave.

The winter solstice snuggles up
to every lover's dreams
but cannot cool the passion of
desire's loving scenes.

Springtime is a rebirth
lovers opening every door
renewing faith in growth and love
settling upon our maudlin core.

the softest touch

I've been to the ditch of night
found no relief in the water
or on the steep banks leading to it.
I've searched the closet of time
where most of our lives are stored
and found nothing there to wear.
I've struggled mightily with the dark
moving through dreams alone
wondering about life without you.

Then I am awakened by your touch
stabilized by all it means to me.
As the equilibrium of my universe
it fills the chambers of my mind
and heart with hope and love
helping me navigate another difficult day
forever grateful that you choose to touch me.

in love's way

Your spirit races reckless, not without you
a brook of love moves warm among
hot rock and shifting sand.
A softness reaching far beyond forever
caressing the silence of my now-extended hand
soon passes behind the noises of tomorrow
where the unknown light of love
is sure to borrow
from a memory of your face upon a pillow
sheltered by the shade of weeping willow
protected by the comfort of my mind.

sharing your view

You hide amidst
     the rocky ledges of unknown
knowing each rock
     and bathing in water
freshly drawn of Nature's tap
     giving sweet to every drop.

You live beside
     the mountain's approach of feeling
for the open sea
     yet know
beyond the sky's expanse
     the changing mood of each vibrant hue.

You feel beside
     love's flirtatious glance
the quaking drama of each lover's grasp
     yet stray not
from wanting
     where others wish to be.

You are the spirit
      never alone
for love has brought you here.
      So don't climb down
except to reach the fulfilling moment
      of bringing me
for I will travel willingly
      home to share your view.

after your light goes out

If your flame died
my candle would flicker.
All other lamps we know would dim
lessening the light
that brightens the way for others
to follow examples you thus established.

insomnia

Let the single light of darkness
swallow shadows from our view.
Let it play its game all night
to give daylight back to you.
From the dark its secrets hide
all things we feel within.
Are the noises first we felt
our selves, just blanched in sin?
Please, let us know what it's about.
Dear God, I think your secret's out!
There's nothing left for us to fear
now that dark is gone
and daylight's here.

this is personal

Your smile is personal.
A vehicle transporting thought
propelling happiness
moving minds and emotion
above the traffic of life
through a sky of hope
drowning all thought exclusive of you.

Your smile
that drives me happily
above the upper half of friendship
into the lower level of love
is also personal
because you know
and travel with me
everywhere I am
anywhere you go.

visionary

My thoughts are of you.
Memory's tired revue leans heavily
upon what we once shared
the love we somehow knew.
Almost alone at times
but not nearly like the feeling
we cried our tears in separate ways
and danced on legs half kneeling.

Your strength a deepened well from which
I filled my cup to drink
to quench despair's thirst for love
moved by what the poets think.
We grew beyond ourselves
our garden verse unrhymed
kept us swaying beyond the season
allowing life 'til now untimed.

Reach out to grasp the hand unknown
tomorrow's melody revealing
the growing path of steps we take
through dewdropped nights' concealing.
Then if our palms enjoin for us
the reason for this jingle
let our lives entwine until
our happiness is single.

in winter in love

Love is an instant replay of hope
living in a holiday of giving
belonging to the mind, residing in the body
expressing itself in tinsel and bright lights.
The beauty of a blackened sky is momentary.
Softened by the thousand colors of blue surrounding it
blessed with age and youth, fresh as footprints in wet snow
it lasts only as long as winter's magic allows.

*I enjoy writing love poems. Writing from personal experience,
imagination, or a combination of both makes it pleasurable.
Seeing love from a different perspective, seeking explanations
through my choice of words...I hope at least to help you think
about the message.*

— R. E. S.

to the future we shall go

We've had our moments in a time of living.
The colors of our tears were unknown to us then.
We shed them without knowing why
but they flowed as sure as rainbows paint the sky
then dry without reason.

We paid the price, not understanding or giving.
Our moment of innocence grew up around us when
we fled from our youth without knowing why.
But what we shared grew like flowers in the landscape
then blossomed out of season.

The test of our future was written in the past
planting in our hearts the seeds we could only wish for
taking years to nurture our separation.
Frequent dawning, soft as fog on a landscape
settling memories as difficult to grasp.

Now we have paid the price patience demands.
When once we gave so willingly without knowing
we are now able to explore the meanings.
The dawn is the revelation that glimmers in this landscape
and we are the rainbows, flowers, fog, and time
waiting to experience togetherness again,

selfless

Some sew
some sing
others mend things
like broken bones or broken hearts.
Whatever you do best
do it for others.

the plane of reason

Savored from embellished
moments of my youth
written upon my embodied soul
each trumpet's blare of truth.
Violate the plane of reason.
Tread certainly through life.
Live beyond wild youth's season
as a threat to
the profane mortality of man.

a visual pot of gold

Contained within moisture and light
often between the storm and sun
a mountain of color chasing vibrancy's might
concentric bands in seamless run.
Moments in time touch every glance
while displayed, in awe we stare
absorbing color's vivid dance.
In silent parade, our hearts are there.

snow

Snow is
winter joy
cheery cheeks
a little boy
hockey sticks
ice that's slick
frozen feet
wet woolen mittens.
All that's neat.
Runny nose
its own identity
Heaven knows
gives moisture to the earth
so all spring flowers
can find their birth.
The spirit of competition
between Nature and God.

San Francisco surprise

I reach without looking
to touch before feeling
sense without knowing
then know before reasoning.
The full of my hand
encircled by fingers
strangely different
momentarily disguised
by lack of recognition
other thoughts prevailing
until drawn together
by your knowing smile.

While attending a fire chiefs' conference in San Francisco, my wife and I, accompanied by two close friends, made a trip to the waterfront. Being engrossed in observation of some trivial pursuit of the moment, it escaped me that my wife and friend had moved on to another area. When I reached casually for my wife's hand without looking up, it was my friend's wife's hand that I took into mine. She immediately realized what I'd done, but instead of pulling away, she decided to wait to see how long before I realized my mistake. She laughed at the moment of recognition. I was both embarrassed and pleased by her joke at my expense. The memory stayed with me nearly twenty years before finding its way into the above poem. It still makes me smile.

— R. E. S.

says who

Invisible hands
that rock my chair
without mood or passion
also send my thoughts
undirected
to unknown destinations
for others to judge
criticize
or enjoy
until the shape of life
meets the terminus
of its existence.

the pause that refreshes

Come join me at the river's edge
to watch the water flow.
Let your mind jump in to ride the current
as far as it can go
past dying fish polluted by
factories lining every shore
beyond darkening aisles of virgin forest
violated long ago
by the hand of man whose presence there
is so difficult to ignore.

Your thoughts can join the melting snow
and gather up the rain
to carry you past lakes and bays
and off to sea again.

Into the clouds, let your mind rise up
from waters deep and cold
within which the winds of current blow
your mind around the world.

Linger now in rainbow's hue
as rain's first kisses pour
to quench the thirst of lily pads
by river's crusty shore.

Drop gently back to earth once more
your body left behind.
Awaken from your moment's rest
to stimulate your mind.

Open up your eyes once more
to what you've witnessed here.
Your mind returns, by now refreshed
by all that you have learned.
As you traveled far away though near
what new passion have you earned?

the old man and the see

A reincarnation of thought
like a catharsis of the mind
I loved everyone in the room
but I can't remember their faces
or which room
or even why I can't remember.

remembering you

I walk upon cement
  or hardwood floors
    while I think of sand
      and seashells
        or footprints on green hills
          and always you are there.

there are gifts in the clearing

My love
you walk from your own tattered tent
across paths overgrown by brambles and brush
disappearing from yourself
and events as yet unattended.

Each footstep taken in new direction
leads you further from cover
yet closer to an expansion of
the fabric from which your tent is made.

Castles can and castles will
designed of cloth or dreams
sometimes unceremoniously tear.
What may be exposed
should be remembered in repair
as love binds in strength
that which should also be forgotten.

Let no voices other than your own
spend time reserved
to release discomfort from trouble's spirit
as it seeks release
from carefully trodden restriction
to clear designs of individual expression.

As you walk in weather never known
across land as yet uncharted
your cadence will quicken when
once again you seek refuge
in that same tattered tent of
comforting self-respect
and all the love it shall remember.

As it shall be remembered
by the gifts you receive
in the clearing
my love.

sands of Key West

A conch shell lying
on the beach
nestled in sand—
a world of memories
within my reach.
As I extend my hand
my youth returns
in darkened tan
a smile upon its face.
Ripples of the past become
tools to interface
connecting memories
dreams first spent
in waves of hope to be
rewarding life
with accomplishment
pertaining now, to me.

    I spent four of the most wonderful years of my life in Key West, Florida. The influence on an individual between eighteen and twenty-two was everlasting. It is where I traveled from youth to manhood. It is where my future was given shape and substance. I am grateful and have never forgotten.

— R. E. S.

know me like i know you

I am the part of night
that seeks the shadows
from moon to ground.
I see clouds move willingly
across the abysmal sky.
I am the ears of night
that listen to trees
sip moisture from the earth.
The sound of quiet glistens
as a chorus of voices—
the manmade voice of God—
sings praises of what
they would want to be.
I am the part of night
they hope to become.
I am nature and a part of you.
I am love.

a lover's toast

Vitality poured freely
from these cups at first
to satisfy nearly unquenchable thirst.
Filled in their purpose
replenished in time
with that which is ours and once was just mine.

To steep in wisdom's continuous flow
the mirror of life does harmonically show
those truthful habits
soon left to drink
imbued in totality by that which we think.

As sweet the bouquet
to our lips soon reveals
beyond every threshold we could possibly feel
from vessel's promise, lately prepared
in blended commitment uniquely shared.

Establish reflections isolated from chance
consenting visions, from dreams' early glance.
The moments together
freshly anointed above
are an unfinished portrait of cascading love.

summer love

A tear crept silently across a tan cheek
to disappear into a sad goodbye.
Loneliness splashed against the cooling sand
where love had lingered
to warm the darkened night.

A sudden empty chill invaded
the early autumn breeze
expressing itself in your absence
as summer's last good-bye
mingled with thoughts of who and why.

A cold rain awakened me
revealing an apparition of our dream.
Without you, without love
emptiness resides in the part of me
where you stay, hidden
insulated from all but my feelings.

winds of love

Like the wind
that rubs the bough
of bending tree
your love gently touches
the depth of my soul
and intensifies my need for you.

just an observation

If a person stays involved
in the surroundings of their world
they will not be surprised
by the changes they observe
nor will they become bored
by their occurrence.

life without you

The sky without clouds
would be empty.
What of the woods
without growing the trees?
The fields so bare
if flowers weren't there
and life without you
without me?

So the breeze pushes clouds
into our view.
The woods replenish in time.
The flowers share company
with sunshine and rain
but life without you
both bitter and blue
is certainly cause for disdain.

The sky would always be empty
the woods growing bleak over time.
The fields ever barren
no flowers to share
darkness sublime
would always be there.

Absent your moments of light
neither I, nor the woods or the flowers
without having you here
could go on with our lives.
The pain would be too hard to bear.

nurturing

Flowers on a window ledge
growing towards the sun
so grows my love
to heaven's height
just knowing
we are one.

self portrait

I'd like to write about love...
Brown eyes
always looking into things
rough hands, gentle and soft
like dispositions you'd admire.
A smile that begins
from holes in the socks
to clear across the chin.
Compassion for seeing
feeling, hearing, touching.
Knowing
the parts of life others ignore.
About ice that melts
because its heart
warms up a subzero day.
About one weed in a garden of flowers.
I'd like to write about all those things
but first
I must compose myself.

    I find this poem very funny. It is because a lot of what I wrote then has changed over the years. Try writing something about yourself in the form of poetry as an exercise to look at a few years later. It's amazing what you leave of yourself on paper.

— *R. E. S.*

time spent loving you

When you want to snuggle
I'll welcome you again
for if you want to cuddle
my arms will hold you in.
Times will be that passion rules
within our emotional venue
projecting passion deeper
than your controls restrict you.
So if we touch each other's heart
to action we can measure
we'll make love, an act of love
that brings resounding pleasure.
But lying here in close embrace
without a fixed agenda
enjoying all you mean to me
is time well spent in splendor.
Reminiscing, laughing, sharing words
about things we like to do
strengthens how I really feel
about time spent loving you.

in the shadow of truth

No one can stand
in the brilliant shadow
of our love
except as a reflection
of its honesty
within the understanding
of its truths.

mirror, mirror on the wall...

Today mirrors tomorrow
with reflections
slow to change.
Cities sleep
in magic shadows
of twinkling light
that disturbs
evening's slumbrous stare
and our sated moment
together.

never alone

If love can turn
at every crossroad
and stop at every sign
if love can race
with speed unchecked
ignoring even time
if love can last
and still be first
can make you hunger
drown your thirst
if love can travel
across the earth
we'll never be alone.

on the steps
of emotional security

When blessings arrive all around us
when blessings abound to surround us
when we recognize it's more than our doing
when we dare to accept truth all-consuming
only then will the compelling role we play
humble the world of our known reality
elevating us to a clear understanding
where the tears so comfortably flow.
Only then will we realize the redemption of
our emotional security
on the steps of a world we must often endure.

in the mist of best wishes

Clouds hung like dreams
on a clothesline of
unlimited imagination.
Dreamers hung on each other
like damp fog on an old suit.
The sun broke through the clouds
and both dreams and dreamers
disappeared like the mist
drying slowly, leaving wrinkles
in the suits of their chosen desires.

lady of the lake and princely frog

The breeze expressed a tender thought
covering you like sweet caress
as from my heart the love it brought
to drape your life in happiness.
Clouds announced my love is real
the sun began to seek its set.
Waves kissed your shore the joy to feel.
At last, our hearts in love have met.

Light in brilliance understood
when first you felt my love for you.
Our ache enjoined as no other could
across the time and distance too.
The wind relaxed to smooth your hair
returned to me its message clear.
'Twas then you knew that I was there
and to my eye it brought a tear.

Some mystery did your love reveal
whispering of emotions felt
in storied tapestry; what you feel
rises like waves above the kelp.
Though we can never touch, to start
keep vigil through each passing night.
Love you feel within your heart
will satisfy need through all its might.
When you are lonely, wanting too
the wind will bring me close to you.

friends

We don't always pick our friends
oftentimes they pick us.
We don't always know the purpose of
friendship
but there *is* a purpose
perhaps hidden from us
until an unspoken need arises
and is satisfied by boundless friendship
in ways we cannot imagine
from those we call our friends.

It would be my pleasure if you enjoyed even one of these poems. You can always let me know, or keep the secret for yourself. In either case, I wish you well as you ponder the message you may have found within my perspective of our world.

— *R. E. S.*

Publisher's note: You can reach R. E. Smith by writing:
Sofa Ink, c/o R. E. Smith, PO Box 65849, Vancouver, WA 98665 or by e-mail to publisher@sofaink.com.

from heart to heart

When you open your mouth to speak
my mind and heart clearly listen.
When you open your mouth to one of my kisses
the music of you fills my soul.
I pay attention, afraid if I don't
I may miss the essence of you.
Too softly, deftly you possess me
for I am the mask you wear every day
when you profess with so many words
Take me as I am.
If only I could take you there
I'd open my mouth and heart to speak.
If only I could speak
it would be a heart to heart discussion.

unrequited love

Is it enough for you
   that I live in the basement
   waiting to be taken up the emotional stairs
   to seek the light of your life again?
How long must I endure
   the silence of a darkened room
   waiting to hear your voice beckoning me
   to share the pleasure of your company
   or the comfort of your once-warm bed?
Where do you keep the touch
   that once reminded me I was never alone?
Or the smile that suggested appreciation
   for just having me near?
Have I become part of your past
   living now in the absence of you?
To not be near you isolates me
   from the world of love.
How much further withdrawn will you become
   before I can no longer reach you?
Even in darkness all I ever wanted
   was to be near you emotionally and physically.
Now the memory grows dim
   without the light we once shared.
How long before the oxygen leaves the corners
   of my darkened room
   smothering the memory of our once-rich love?

lifeguard

Motion and sun kiss water and wind.
They share a blanket of hope with which each is covered.
Love, a sleeping ocean, awakened when
warm fingers caress deep secrets.

They share a blanket of hope with which each is covered
spread across the expansive emotion loving creates.
Tears fall gently from the face of ecstasy.
Knowing eyes awaken, limpid glistening jewels.

Spread across the expansive emotion loving creates
lovers embrace the moment of awakening.
Undulating waves reach inward to affect feelings
resting placidly in this liquid heart.

Lovers embrace the moment of awakening
languishing in thoughts of magic proclaimed
looking forward to basking in the sun of their creation
saved again from drowning in solitude's empty tears.

vignettes minus words

I'm busy uniting bits of life, parts of dreams.
Collecting memories, vignettes minus words
pieces of special moments found in their seams
imagination of ages, waiting to be heard.

Revisiting people at work or at play
candid imprints of emotional calm.
Interacting with others in a special way
leaving themselves a legacy, an essential balm.

Pulling together feelings and expectations
from people's unresolved notions
becoming a voice to help release tension
with hope applied as sympathetic lotion.

Gathering babies' smiles, solitary tears
accompanied by anguished sobs of pain
the shock of silence extending the years
that a lover's goodbye can never explain.

Busy again savoring love's tender touches
the hopeful look of questioning eyes
the playful glance of innocent flirtation
a momentary pleasure of sweetened surprise.

108

Savoring a breeze expressed to inform
a respite from even blistering heat
or drops of rain from a pending storm
that puddles leisurely at our feet.

broken interlude

Adagio guitar notes
tugged from a melancholy heart.
Music prepared to bleed sweet nectar
from the first note
played to deaf ears, an emotional tune.
Strumming chords we both once knew
songs of surrender, where love had been.
Then the curtain fell on our cabaret
where loneliness echoed in repose.
Hollow applause lingered
long into the night.

the clouds of romance

When the sun shines hard on shadows cast
when music plays soft of memories past
when mood reflects images of happier times
when bells toll truth in resounding chimes
only then will clouds of desperation clear
only then will lovers surely hear.

Hearts then will open to what lies ahead
comfort will be found in a once-soft bed.

So if you find the place warmed by the sun
where songs play on, never seemingly done
mirrored in reasons to bring out your smile
with trust the bellwether mile after mile
on a windswept path of a journey together
your love will then last, in spite of the weather.

above all else

Beyond the loft
above the vane
surpass all clouds
before the rain
begins the blue
starts a light
that signals day
or cautions night.
Where thoughts will go
when dreams abound
all love begins
above the ground.
There gently shakes
in all its mirth
a passive glow
reaching earth.
The soul radiating
from the sky
molding life
for you and I.

lost in common

A face with only eyes
beseeching me in my dream
wanting to be heard.
Eyes said it all
and I listened.
The eyes smiled
comforting me
until they shed tears—
droplets of hope, not want.
Somehow I knew.
The eyes saw *me* and understood.
We communicated
becoming lost in common
in thought
in vision
until I was awakened.

psychological terror

As a rabbit in a root, dwarfed
by the immensity of my surroundings
suspicious of my place in the overwhelming darkness
of shadows cast upon the ground.
I hide in terror from movement in the woods
afraid to stay in
more fearful of venturing out
starving from indecision
and a terminal case of fear.

tragedy remembered, 2005...
of sweet promised times, 1963

More than books were deposited
to be immortalized that November afternoon.
High on a grassy knoll
a shot echoed in protest
made its mark on history's page
recorded as a moment of mystery
framed in question and deepening doubt.

For no matter how many times
we review the replay
it won't change the outcome.
Answer the question
or fill the void
of what might have been.
A nation still weeps.
The world tries desperately to recover
from the never-fading memory
or events of change.

in the beginning...

Before the dawn of time unyielding
before the reign of winter's cold
before the moment's first revealing
before the loss of love grown old
there lived a moment sparked in pleasure
there a life unto its own
there the hope of simple treasure
there a dream of rapture known.
In the wind of ash, dust, and sulphur
spores drifted off first to sow.
In that moment, prophesied forever
in the smile of God, the world began to grow.

reaching our destiny

The slowly forming key
turns to affix itself
to the destiny
prepared for every man's soul.

The past from which we run
or wait to catch us never will
for its travel is in opposite direction
from our view and destination.

The famed broadcast of life
remains a dilemma
that will be replayed in the mind of man
forever.

love is born

Ice cracked the rock.
Music melted ice.
Heat molded stone
then joined sand and sea
into perfect union of precious thought.
A relationship of fortune
yielding to happiness, honesty
from earth and sea
red clay and green grass.
Love is born.
Shared in each of us
known to ourselves by every tree
and step of path along the way.
Colors watched, elements whispered.
Mystery danced to entertain
while learning to believe
the reality of every dream
and each other.

the keys to our past

There are keys
that unlock forgotten pictures
of fathers' pride, mothers' happiness.
Drawers of family thought
puzzles of yesterday
colors of Christmas
mirrors of time.
Reflections of hope for some
despair for others
whose doors stay locked
because they have lost the key
on their way to the door.

waiting

(a moment of time for a lifetime of moments)

In the music of the mountain
on the moment that we shared
in the whispered waves
surrounded by the island of *I cared*.
In the rounded edge of ice and snow
surviving in the streams
on the soul of life's serenity
and knowing what that means.
In the pawnshop of the fragrant truth
from beds where flowers grow
where love begins, please wait for me
above the earthly show.
Aware that life is waiting now
as answer to our call
if I hadn't been here with you
I would not have been at all.

the rainbow's end

Beyond the pond
of pleasant thought
into the sea of Man
the author of structured time
the hope of outstretched hand.

the emergence of the elderly

The pictures I'm looking at are not of my youthful friends.
They are of two aged dinosaurs sharing a grin.
What happened to slim faces surrounded by dark, wavy curls?
Gone with the ages, and the outlook is grim.
How many more years will we be privileged to share?
The exuberance diminished to an occasional demand
what once was the exception of natural display, is
now the picture showing lines of demarcation
and years of adventuresome travel over hard roads of learning.
Pain and joy are not recognized in the faces seen here.
I wouldn't recognize either of them on the street if we met
and yet etched in the lines and creases they bear
in the gray beards and well-fed faces of experience
is the honor of true friendship. They are older now
but still friends. That much is crystal clear.
I see as much through my own dinosaur eyes and smile through
my own gray beard at the pleasure their picture brings me.

moments before the maelstrom

Our lives are like clouds within a cloud
at times surrounded by enveloping dynamics.
Energy and motion control our destiny.
Other times we enjoy brilliance contributing
to the beauty of the pending storm.
Seen by others as the center of magnificence portrayed
by the presence we bring to the reality of the moment
it is only then we become part of the silver lining
people recall about the portrait within their view.

a world of our own

Where are we going?
Together.
What will we find there?
Each other.
How long will we be there?
Forever.
How will we know we've arrived?
We'll be there.
How will we get there?
Only, in love.

all you mean to me

You take me places I can't go alone
where the harmony of angels' voices
echoes in my heart.
You show me things I'd otherwise be
too blind to see
without the glow your delicate radiance manifests.
I'd be adrift on an ocean of uncertainty
absent the buoyancy of
your shared spirit.
You are the goddess of my dreams
the breath of my life.
Missing you fills my mouth with
the unfamiliar taste of bitterroot.
You are my everything.
To lose you is more frightening
than facing the certainty of my own demise.
Your loss would leave
a table once full of sweet dessert
a banquet of desire, empty
of all but memory.
The verity of my love for you is real
undeniable and eternal
created by the breath of God
in the blessing bestowed upon us.

daddy's little girl

Child of beauty
morning bright
daylight leaps from your smile.
It fills the room
with the innocent
softness of your eyes.
You touch my heart.
Your words like fingers
caress my very soul.
You step into experience
with wholesome hope
and fearless vulnerability.
No longer the budding flower
you are now a beautiful rose
yet you are still a child, ready
to become a bouquet of life.

a blending view

The sun's early glances
blush the mountain in rouge
while the poet's pen
drains the embarrassed clouds
of morning light
to fill the amplified quiet
with a burning cold dawn
disturbed only by the occasional
intruding thought of man
who contemplates the immensity
of God's design
and kisses Nature's cheek
in consideration of
the blending portrait.

are we there yet?

When do we know if we are traveling in the right direction
on a road where we are unaware of beginning or end
or compass points to reveal which way the road travels?
Too many people stand in the middle of the road
on a line of indecision, afraid of moving either way
for fear of getting lost, when the fools are already lost
by an inability to build on the progress of a first step.

*Thank you for spending some time at this crossroads to share
together. May friends and love propel you to a successful voyage.
I hope your tasks will not be burdensome and that we might
meet again to share and reflect.*

— R. E. S.

Poems Alphabetically by Title

Poems by Theme

Loss

Love

About the Author

The love of his family, augmented with the human intensity of a long career as a fire chief, have given R. E. Smith a rich fountain of inspiration from which he draws to write his poems.

Already a regional celebrity for both his written word and gentle skill at sharing and storytelling, R. E. Smith is also an award-winning poet and writer. He is currently working on both another collection of poetry and a novel.

Between writing and speaking engagements, he enjoys life in the Pacific Northwest with his wife Bonne and six cats.